Original title:
Finding Purpose One Coffee at a Time

Copyright © 2025 Creative Arts Management OÜ
All rights reserved.

Author: Alexander Thornton
ISBN HARDBACK: 978-1-80566-243-3
ISBN PAPERBACK: 978-1-80566-538-0

Reflection Over Roasting

Steam rises high, oh what a sight,
Beans dance and whirl, in morning light.
A sip of magic, just a taste,
Life's big questions, no time to waste.

Beware the caffeine, it plays a trick,
Suddenly thoughts are zooming quick.
What's my purpose? I take a sip,
And laugh at life's wild, jittery trip.

Rich Brews, Richer Lives

Brew it strong, with laughter loud,
Fill the cup and join the crowd.
With each rich sip, I chase my dream,
Life's a joke, or so it seems.

Coffee spills, and so do words,
Mixing life with playful curds.
From foamy tops to hearty chuckles,
Joy's brewed here with all our snuggles.

Savoring Small Successes

One mug down, I feel the cheer,
With every gulp, I face the fear.
Small wins stack like spoonfuls sweet,
Caffeine and giggles, life's real treat.

Every drip a little grace,
Me and my dreams, we embrace.
A latte here, an espresso shot,
Turning woes to laughter, a whole lot!

Cuppa Joy

A frothy crown atop my brew,
Each cup brings smiles, that's my cue.
From drowsy morn to lively noon,
I lift my mug and sing a tune.

Here's to the days that start with foam,
With every sip, I feel at home.
The world may spin, but I just sip,
Life's an adventure, let's take a trip.

Sipped Epiphanies

With each cup, I ponder loud,
Dreams bubble up, like frothy cloud.
My coffee mug, a trusty guide,
Stirring thoughts I cannot hide.

Beneath the steam, ideas bloom,
Like morning sun that chases gloom.
I sip and grin, my woes in tow,
Life's mysteries, like espresso flow.

Brews and Beginnings

Each morning starts with a brew,
A ritual, both old and new.
With beans and laughter, I conspire,
Every sip ignites my fire.

A dash of cream, a sprinkle fun,
In this cup, great tales begun.
Laughing loud, I spill my fate,
Decisions made in coffee's gait.

Whispers of the Roaster

The roaster whispers secrets bold,
In every cup, a story told.
I perk up with each fragrant whiff,
Life's quirks served with a silly riff.

As beans collide in swirls of cheer,
I find my muse with every career.
Brewed adventures start and thrive,
In caffeine dreams, we come alive.

The Daily Grind of Self

Every grind holds a tale to share,
Awake, alert, without a care.
With silly grins and frothy cheer,
I brew my thoughts while dreaming near.

With coffee grounds, my soul takes flight,
Chasing laughs into the night.
Each sip a giggle, a playful tease,
In rhythmic swirls, I find my ease.

Heartbeats in a Carafe

Pour me some joy, my morning brew,
With every sip, I feel brand new.
The caffeine dance, a waltz of cheer,
I laugh at life, my vision clear.

In a cup of beans, my thoughts take flight,
I muse on dreams, both day and night.
A splash of cream, the sugar swirls,
Life's conundrums turn into pearls.

Brewed hope brews bold with every grind,
I brew solutions I didn't find.
A latte laugh, a cappuccino sigh,
My purpose here? Just caffeinate and fly!

So fill my cup, let's raise a cheer,
For every sip, my path is clear.
With every clink, we toast the good,
In coffee we trust, as best we could.

One Sip Closer to Clarity

Wake up, sleepyhead, join the grind,
With the liquid gold, wisdom I'll find.
A drop of laughter, a splash of glee,
   Sipping my way to serenity.

Steam rises high, like dreams unmade,
In this cozy mug, ambitions invade.
Espresso shot, I'm on my way,
To conquer the world, at least today!

Chocolate sprinkles and swirling froth,
In this caffeinated chaos, I'm never doth.
A sip of joy, a hiccup of thrills,
With every gulp, I scribble my wills.

So hand me that mug, let's raise our brows,
Finding humor in life, and laughter avows.
With every sip, I wiggle and spark,
   My coffee routine? It's quite the art!

Savoring the Now

In the morning light, I brew,
Caffeine dreams dance into view.
Sipping joy in every drop,
Watch my sleepy self just hop.

Mug in hand, I take a swig,
Awakening with every gig.
Frothy foam atop my treat,
A little latte makes me neat.

Warmth in a Mug

Oh, the warmth from my fine cup,
Feels like a great big cozy hug.
As the steam rises up high,
I pretend I can touch the sky.

Each sip brings a little cheer,
Chasing away the daily drear.
With every gulp, I crack a grin,
Who knew joy could come from within?

Journey Through the Grounds

Exploring beans from far and wide,
Roasted tales I cannot hide.
Epic quests in every brew,
Adventure calls, and I pursue.

Grinding, pouring, making mess,
Come on, caffeine, I'm in distress!
With the magic of this blend,
Every moment feels like a friend.

Liquid Light

Coffee's glow, a warm delight,
Fueling dreams into the night.
Cracking jokes as I take a sip,
A little giggle on my trip.

It's the sunshine in my mug,
A perky dance, a little tug.
Every sip, a smile ignites,
Who knew morning could feel so bright?

Pouring Clarity

In the morning light, I brew my fate,
The coffee warms, it doesn't wait.
Each sip's a joke, a punchline brewed,
Life's absurd, but I'm in the mood.

With every drip, my thoughts take flight,
Like caffeinated birds, oh what a sight!
A latte laugh, a cappuccino grin,
Who knew caffeine could make me win?

The mug's my stage, the steam my cue,
Life's comedy wrapped in a cup or two.
With every pour, my worries fade,
Is that profound, or just the upgrade?

So here I sip, and giggle slightly,
World's a joke, and it feels just right.
I raise my mug to the morning sun,
A brew of cheer, and I am done!

Percolating Thoughts

Beans grinding loud, a morning song,
Percolating dreams, where I belong.
With frothy milk and sugar's embrace,
I craft my plans, at my own pace.

The kettle's dance, a funny ballet,
As time ticks on, it's coffee play.
A sip of bold, a dash of cheer,
Suddenly life's less severe.

Thoughts bubble up like foam on top,
Each idea brewed, I just can't stop.
What's the plan? I haven't a clue,
But this cup's a muse, it's funny too!

So let it steep, let the laughter grow,
Around this mug, good vibes will flow.
With every taste, bold flavors call,
I'll brew my joy, and have a ball!

A Journey in Every Brew

Each morning's trek begins with beans,
A flavorful map of coffee scenes.
A sip takes me to places grand,
With every brew, I'm off, just planned.

From Colombia's hills to Ethiopia's sun,
As flavors dance, my worries run.
A mocha mountain or a latte lake,
In every cup, a chance to wake.

The journey's wild, but laughter leads,
The steam rises, fulfilling needs.
With humor served alongside the cream,
I toast to life, and dare to dream.

So join this trip, grab a mug so bright,
Let's wander far, from morning to night.
In every cup, there's a story spun,
From coffee quests, we all have fun!

The Quiet Morning Medley

In the dawn's hush, I brew my tune,
With coffee notes, I wake up soon.
A splash, a sip, the day comes alive,
A symphony brewed, where giggles thrive.

Espresso shots and a frothy swirl,
Each morning dance makes my head whirl.
The kettle's chirp, like a morning bird,
A funny start, that's what I've heard.

As I indulge in grounds and steam,
I find my focus, I chase a dream.
The laughter bubbles, the jokes run free,
Who knew coffee's so therapeutic, whee!

Quiet moments shared, one sip at a time,
Each laughter echoed feels like a rhyme.
With every cup, the morning parade,
A medley of joy, in each cascade!

The Warmth Within

In a cup, this magic brews,
A jolt of joy, no time to snooze.
Sipping slowly, life's a game,
Who knew a latte could bring fame?

Frothy foam, a smile it makes,
With every sip, my soul awakes.
Life is better, come what may,
When caffeine points me on my way.

Savoring Epiphanies

A drip, a drop, my thoughts unfold,
With every sip, new dreams take hold.
Eureka! From my java cup,
Ideas swirl, I can't give up.

Espresso shots, they fire my brain,
With every blend, there's much to gain.
Caffeine kicks to fuel my schemes,
Pour some more—let's chase those dreams!

The Mug of Motivation

In my hands, a vessel bright,
Once so dull, now pure delight.
Caffeine magic in each swirl,
Turning chaos into pearl.

Every sip, my spirits sing,
Life's a dance, and coffee's the king.
With latte art, I craft my fate,
Caffeine dreams, I cannot wait!

Stirring the Spirit

Brewed for growth, my daily grind,
Stirring thoughts, it's all aligned.
A sprinkle of joy, a dash of fun,
Watch me shine, the day's begun!

With every cup, I find my groove,
A comedy show in every move.
Caffeine on the daily, that's my jam,
With laughter brewed, who gives a damn?

Sips of Clarity

I brew a pot, my heart's on fire,
Each splash, a thought, my mind's desire.
A latte swirl, my genius peek,
With whipped cream doodles, I feel unique.

Brewed dreams dance in steaming cups,
Mug in hand, I build my ups.
My daily grind, a playful tease,
Coffee's spell brings thoughts with ease.

Java Journeys

With every sip, I plot my course,
Drifting dreams from caffeine's force.
Beneath the foam, my plans unfold,
Exploring life, both brave and bold.

Espresso shots, like magic wands,
Turn sleepy heads into great bands.
From bean to brew, strange tales arise,
In every cup, a sweet surprise.

Caffeine Dreams

In steaming cups, my thoughts unite,
Fluffy clouds, oh what a sight!
With every sip, I chase the sun,
Coffee dreams, we're on the run!

A mocha muse, a cappuccino cheer,
With frothy chaos, I steer my sphere.
Perks of life, oh how they gleam,
Fueling my wildest, wackiest dream.

The Elixir of Discovery

A mug of joy, my daily fix,
With every sip, I pull the tricks.
Drips of wisdom from filters fine,
Transforming thoughts in coffee line.

Shaken not stirred, my brews collide,
With every gulp, new dreams I ride.
The secret lies in how I sip,
Discovery's dance in this caffeine trip.

Rituals in a Mug

Each morning starts with a clink,
A dance with beans, no time to think.
The kettle sings, the mug awaits,
A liquid hug, it never grates.

With frothy smiles and sugar sprinkles,
I sip the joys, as laughter crinkles.
My daily quest, oh what a treat,
To caffeinate my busy feet.

The swirl of cream, a masterpiece,
In sips I find my inner peace.
Yet spills abound, I wear a stain,
But coffee's charm eases the pain.

So raise your cup, toast with glee,
To caffeine's magic, wild and free.
In every drop, a giggle flows,
With every cup, joy overflows.

The Barista's Philosophy

Behind the counter, wisdom brews,
A shot of espresso, the wake-up muse.
With every grind, a lesson learned,
In spilled cups, my patience earned.

I craft each latte with a grin,
A foam heart formed, let humor win.
As customers sip, their worries fade,
In coffee steam, new dreams are laid.

The world's a blend of sweet and bitter,
Just like my drink that makes you glitter.
So take a sip, embrace the fun,
For life's too short when you're on the run.

Remember, dear friend, don't just consume,
Let each sip dance, let laughter bloom.
Life's frothy foam, enjoy the swirl,
With each espresso, let laughter unfurl.

Lattes and Life Lessons

A latte art that speaks so loud,
A frothy heart, I feel so proud.
With every sip, a lesson shared,
In caffeine buzz, I'm truly bared.

Creamy whispers in a cozy mug,
Stirring life where dreams can snug.
I sip my way through ups and downs,
In every cup, a wisdom crowns.

Each flavor tells a funny tale,
With every gulp, I start to sail.
So nervous sips turn bold and bright,
In coffee's embrace, we find our light.

So here's to mugs of joy and zest,
In every drop, I find my quest.
Let laughter brew and froth arise,
For life's a laugh in every sigh.

The Aromatic Journey

On this journey, I take a ride,
With aromatic beans as my guide.
Each morning whiff, a sweet embrace,
In swirling steam, I find my place.

The world can wait, just one more sip,
A caffeine hug, a gentle trip.
I lose myself in mocha dreams,
Where chocolate rivers flow in streams.

From bean to brew, my heart does race,
With every slurp, a silly face.
Oh how I dance with flavors bold,
In every cup, a story told.

So grab your mugs, let laughter flow,
For coffee magic is quite the show.
Join me on this aromatic spree,
Where every sip brings joy and glee.

Grounded Moments

Early morning brew, a wake-up call,
Staring at grounds, I ponder it all.
Why am I here? What's the deal?
Is it just caffeine, or something surreal?

Sips of magic in a porcelain mug,
With each gulp, I feel a cozy hug.
Conversations with foam, so lofty and grand,
Making plans with a half-caffeinated hand.

Muffins join in as the plot thickens,
While donuts wink, as my journal quickens.
Every sip opens my cluttered mind,
In search for wisdom, it's coffee I find.

Life's little puzzles mix with the cream,
Baffling questions float like a dream.
A cup of laughter, a dash of zest,
Who knew a brew could be such a quest?

The Flavor of Enlightenment

Dark roast whispers secrets anew,
As light dances in my caffeinated view.
Espresso shots pierce through the haze,
Enlightenment comes in a caffeinated craze.

A latte laughs, frothy and bright,
While I ponder my past in the morning light.
Do the beans know? Do they conspire?
To awaken my soul with their gentle fire?

Every stir is a thought, a marvelous spree,
Searching for answers, just me and my tea.
Brewing wisdom, with every slurp,
I sip on joy, and the questions burp.

From long black nights to the drip of dawn,
A quest for meaning, I'll carry on.
With each coffee break, a spark ignites,
In the flavor of life, I find my delights.

Coffee Break Revelations

In the café corner, I take a seat,
Eyes on the barista, she's hard to beat.
As I wait for a cup, I reflect on the day,
Does my agenda need more frothy display?

Caffeine confessions flow like a stream,
With cappuccino dreams, I plot and scheme.
Maybe it's all in the foam art design,
That sparks my thoughts, oh how divine!

Sugar packets open like secrets untold,
Stirring up plans that are daring and bold.
With every sip, my worries combust,
In caffeine, I find both madness and trust.

The timer's ticking, I sip with intent,
A coffee break whispers, "Be well, be content."
As laughter surrounds in a fragrant embrace,
Revelations arise with frothed-up grace.

Seamless Steeps

Tea leaves quiver in boiling delight,
Steeping my thoughts in the afternoon light.
Chai spice dances, a fragrant ballet,
While I ponder the meaning of life, come what may.

Brewed with a wink, my kettle hums low,
Each droplet whispers, 'Let your spirit flow.'
In every steep, a quirky idea,
Like how I once wore socks with flip-flops, oh dear!

A sip of green wisdom, a splash of new tales,
In this teacup world, my laughter prevails.
Life bubbles over, steeped in a giggle,
As I watch in awe, my worries wiggle.

Let's face the day, with jade sips galore,
In a blend of flavors, who could want more?
With each seamless steep, I discover my cheer,
In the whimsical world of my sweet, brewed beer.

The Search in Every Sip

In a cup, I seek a sign,
A latte god, divine and fine.
Espresso dreams and frothy hopes,
My morning muse in mugs and ropes.

With every sip, a giggle grows,
Like cream that swirls, the whimsy flows.
One sip, I ponder life anew,
In caffeine's grip, what else to do?

Stirring Up Purpose

Stirring dreams with every brew,
A spoonful of joy, a dash of rue.
I whirl my thoughts, and who knows what?
A coffee shop's my thinking hut.

Beans of wisdom roast and grind,
In cracked cups, I hope to find,
A sparkle in the sleepy haze,
A purpose brewed in coffee's blaze.

The Coffee Canvas

A canvas stained with mocha flair,
Splashing laughter everywhere.
My brush, a spoon, my palette brown,
Pouring joy in every town.

With every drip, a color flows,
In frothy swirls, my laughter grows.
I paint my days with beans so bold,
In every sip, a story told.

Mornings of Meaning

Mornings bright with caffeine cheer,
As I down my cup, I commandeer.
Each gulp a giggle, each drop a dream,
In steamy cups, I'll surely beam.

The microwave hums a joyful tune,
As I craft my bliss with every swoon.
Brewed revelations, hot and strong,
In morning's light, I hum along.

Sip by Sip: The Search

In the café, I take a seat,
Dreaming big, my life's retreat.
With a latte froth and a smile,
Maybe purpose is just a mile.

I sip and ponder, is it real?
Is my ticket out an espresso deal?
The barista nods, my muse divine,
Her winks say, 'Just be a grapevine!'

A Steaming Soul

My cup's in hand, I take a chance,
With every gulp, I start to dance.
Is this the brew that sets me free?
Or just caffeine's bold jubilee?

The steam rises like thoughts on high,
I could save the world—or just sigh.
In every sip, a giggle bubbles,
Coffee clarity amidst the troubles.

Mug Meditations

In morning light, I raise my mug,
Awake and wide, snug as a bug.
This cup of joy, my gentle guide,
A liquid hug I cannot hide.

With every swirl, my thoughts take flight,
Mixing dreams with a dash of fright.
Here's to the chaos yet the fun,
Amidst the froth, my life's a pun!

Pure Intent in Every Pour

The barista pours with flair and style,
Each drip and drop takes a while.
I sip my drink, pretend to plot,
'Cause who needs plans? I'll take a shot!

In coffee's depths, I see reflections,
Of goals and dreams with no directions.
But hey, let's raise a mug and cheer,
For in this chaos, purpose is near!

The Art of Percolation

In a pot, my dreams do boil,
A dance of grounds, a fragrant toil.
Each drip, a chuckle, each sip, a grin,
Life's little joys brewed deep within.

Mornings spill with laughter loud,
As coffee spills, I feel so proud.
Espresso shots, a jolt of cheer,
My caffeine muse brings purpose near.

I juggle mugs with grace unmatched,
My latte art? It's all quite hatched.
A swan or heart, a woeful hare,
All created in my morning care.

So raise a cup, let's toast and cheer,
With every sip, let's conquer fear.
For in this brew, we laugh and play,
Each cup, a step towards sunny day.

Reflections in a Café

Sipping slowly, I glance around,
The café buzz, a joyful sound.
Baristas dance like pros with flair,
While customers pretend to care.

I spy a dad with toddler near,
His coffee's gone, but still, no fear.
He smiles as juice goes flying high,
His latte's safe—how, oh, why?

A pondered life in every mug,
A caffeinated, frothy hug.
With giggles shared, I claim a seat,
Where whimsy makes my heart skip beat.

The steam and laughter intertwine,
A daily dose, a silly sign.
In coffee shops, we find our bliss,
One sip away from joy's sweet kiss.

Daily Rituals of Hope

Upon the counter, grounds cascade,
Each morning brew, a playful trade.
A dance of flavors, a twist of fate,
Today's agenda—just hold on, wait!

With every pour, the worries fade,
My insulated cup, a trusty aid.
Each sip a whisper, 'You'll be fine!'
Life's riddles solved in dark roast wine.

I fumble with the cream and sugar,
In this ballet, I become a slumber.
Flip-flops, stains, and a crooked cap,
Yet somehow, I still map my path.

Here's to the mornings, wild and free,
With mugs that sing of possibility.
A daily laugh, a hopeful nod,
My brew-filled journey shaped by God.

The Language of Lattes

In frothy swirls, our tales unfold,
Each cup, a story waiting bold.
With a sprinkle of cocoa, I spin my fate,
Chronicles brewed in a porcelain state.

A dash of wit, and here we go,
Espresso feelings overflow.
These little cups, they speak to me,
With whispers rich of irony.

To latte art, I raise my hand,
Crafting portraits that don't quite stand.
Swans and tulips, oh so awry,
Still, they grin, as if saying, 'Try!'

So toast your dreams, give them a sip,
In this café, let my joy equip.
Each milky wave, a gentle cheer,
In every latte, purpose clear.

The Aftertaste of Ambition

In the mug of dreams, I dive,
A swirl of cream to keep me alive.
Ambition's brew, with a dash of bliss,
Every sip whispers, 'You can't miss!'

Chasing goals like a caffeine high,
With each gulp, I aim for the sky.
But sometimes I spill, oh what a mess!
That's just passion's way to confess!

Friends gather round for a caffeinated chat,
Stirring up schemes, and a little chit-chat.
Life's a latte, frothy and bright,
Together we stir, we take flight!

So here's to the grind and the coffee spills,
To caffeinated laughter and giddy thrills.
With every sip, I raise my cup,
To all the dreams that bubble up!

Steamy Visions

Steam rising up like dreams in my head,
Coffee visions dance while I'm still in bed.
A splash of laughter in my morning brew,
Who needs a plan when my latte's in view?

I ponder my days while the espresso flows,
Imagining life like a coffee rose.
Each cup a canvas, each sip a chance,
In the cafe of life, I do my dance.

With whipped cream clouds and chocolate dreams,
I craft my stories with frothy themes.
Barista of fate, mix my fate please,
In this jazzy blend, I find my ease.

So raise your mug, let the laughter spill,
In each aromatic drop, we find the thrill.
Life's a comedy brewed, no need to grieve,
With every sip, there's more to believe!

Brewed Reflections

In the morning light, I brew my fate,
Reflecting on life while I caffeinate.
Sipping on dreams like a creamy blend,
Wishing each cup wouldn't come to an end.

My thoughts bubble up like hot espresso,
What's next? Who knows? Let's go with the flow.
I sketch my plans through a steamy haze,
Finding clarity in the milky maze.

Each mug a moment, a pause to ponder,
In this coffee shop, I let thoughts wander.
Sipping and smiling, the world feels right,
Buzzing with ideas, I take flight!

So here's to the brews and the brains that churn,
Finding wisdom in each sip I learn.
Life's wisdom flows in this java song,
With every cup, I feel I belong!

Finding Meaning in Each Drop

A drop of coffee, a splash of joy,
Brewing hope like a favorite toy.
Stirring dreams in a porcelain cup,
With every sip, I can't give up!

Beneath the foam and the dark cascade,
I seek the magic in every trade.
From bitter to sweet, life's rich taste,
I laugh at the mess, there's no need for haste.

Each cup a chapter, a sitcom scene,
Where laughter bubbles and life's serene.
With friends by my side, we sip and grin,
In this mug of life, let's dive right in!

So raise your cup to the dreamy spree,
In every drop lies the key to be free.
Savor the moments with frothy cheer,
For life's a latte, and we've no time to fear!

Steaming Ambitions

With a cup in hand, I start my day,
Dreams go brewing, come what may.
Espresso shots and latte art,
Fueling ambitions that warm my heart.

As I sip, new ideas sprout,
Caffeine whispers, 'Give life a shout!'
Each sip's a chance, a quest to chase,
I'm a barista in a dreams' embrace.

My coffee's hot, my thoughts run wild,
A jolt of joy, like a carefree child.
Pour another round, let's seize the scene,
In this café of life, I reign as queen.

So cheers to mugs and frothy highs,
With every gulp, I touch the skies.
Who knew the brew could lead the way?
In laughter and cream, I find my play.

Java Journeys

A sip of joy, a taste of glee,
Java dreams dance, so carefree.
With beans so bold, my spirit swells,
In every cup, a tale compels.

I wander through cafés, cup in tow,
Each brew a path, come join the flow!
With every slurp, I catch a grin,
These coffee adventures make me spin.

A caramel swirl, a mocha blast,
In this caffeine journey, I'll have a blast!
From cappuccinos to iced delights,
Every flavor lifts me to new heights.

As cream swirls round, laughter brews,
I sip on fun, no time to snooze.
So here's to laughter, life, and beans,
In every cup, a world of dreams.

Deep Brews and Dreams

In a deep cup, I dip my hopes,
Stirring dreams, as happiness elopes.
Each sip ignites a roar of cheer,
Brewing laughter, year after year.

From frothy tops to hearty grounds,
In every mug, adventure abounds!
I'll sip and conquer, laugh out loud,
With a coffee grin, I feel so proud.

The world's my café, the barista me,
Crafting memories, carefree and free.
With chocolate shavings and cinnamon dust,
I find my way, in coffee I trust.

So pour me a cup, let's sip til dawn,
In this liquid magic, we'll carry on.
Each brew is a chapter, a story divine,
Holding my dreams in a java shrine.

Caffeine Chronicles

Gather round for a tale so tall,
Of caffeine adventures that befall.
With every cup, a new plot twist,
A comedy where no laugh's missed.

From morning brews to evening drip,
Every mocha's like a friendship trip.
Caramel swirls and whipped cream clouds,
I sip up joy, it always draws crowds.

The grind of the beans is like life's race,
But with laughter and love, it's a merry chase.
So let's caffeinate and conquer the day,
In this whimsical tale, we laugh our way!

With mugs raised high, let's toast to cheer,
Each sip a giggle, with friends so dear.
So grab your cup, it's time to embark,
In this caffeine story, we leave our mark.

Reflections in Each Sip

In the bottom of my cup, I see,
Dreams of who I hope to be,
With each swirl, my thoughts take flight,
Espresso shots ignite the night.

Lattes whisper, secrets bold,
Tales of life yet to unfold,
Sugar cubes dance, a sweet little lie,
As I ponder why I even try.

My mug, it tells a funny tale,
Of attempts that flopped, and those that sailed,
Every sip a giggle, a wry smile,
Stimulates my thoughts, at least a while.

So here's to mornings, warm and bright,
With every cup, I feel the light,
In frothy foam, I find my grin,
Who knew purpose brewed from within?

The Heartbeat of a Roast

Roasting beans in a merry dance,
Filling my mug, giving life a chance,
With each drip and splash, a rhythm flows,
A caffeinated heartbeat, goodness glows.

I slurp and sip, a joyous sound,
With coffee magic, I'm tightly bound,
Caramel swirls of giggly fate,
In every cup, the world's first date.

Barista's tricks, a circus show,
Whipped cream tops, in laughter, we flow,
As I ponder my life in caffeine streams,
With every sip, I chase my dreams.

So pour me a shot of that dark delight,
As I solve the mysteries of my plight,
One laugh, one coffee, all in good fun,
Finding my path while I sip and run.

Brewed Beginnings

Morning ritual, the grind begins,
As I wait for that first sip, I grin,
A coffee ceremony, holy and bright,
Start my day with a jolt, pure delight.

Cups stacked high, like a tower of cheer,
Every blend whispers, "Come sit near,"
I ponder my fate with a frothy top,
In a latte world, I never stop.

Sips of joy, the laughter flows,
Coffee talk, where anything goes,
In a mocha haze, I find my call,
One sip away from conquering all.

Cheers to the beans, oh what a ride,
As caffeine guides and I glide,
In every sip, a little spark,
Filling up life's great big park.

Coffee Shop Confessions

In a cozy nook where secrets spill,
I confess my plans, both grand and shrill,
With every brew, my worries dissolve,
As I sip and ponder my life to evolve.

Sugar sweet lies play on my tongue,
While the espresso sings, oh so young,
Behind steam clouds, the truth takes form,
Each cup a chance to weather the storm.

Laughter bounces off tiled walls,
Between the sips, my heart recalls,
Funny quirks of my daily grind,
Over steamed milk, new paths I find.

So raise your mug, let's toast to fate,
With every cup, let's celebrate,
For in this café, we all unwind,
It's here that purpose is lovingly designed.

The Ritual of Reflection

Every morning I rise with a quest,
My bedhead a crown, I'm not at my best.
With coffee in hand, I dive into thought,
Is this a good life, or just what I bought?

I sip and I ponder, my mug feels like gold,
Each grain of ground wisdom, carefully told.
With each little gulp, my worries take flight,
Is today the day I'll finally get it right?

Driven by caffeine, my dreams start to bloom,
Can a cup of joe really lighten the gloom?
Mix in some laughter, a dash of delight,
In this café of life, I'm the star of the night.

So here's to my brew, my dear morning friend,
With each little sip, my troubles will end.
I lift up my mug with a cheeky little grin,
Cheers to the chaos — let this day begin!

Finding Direction in Brewed Beans

In my quirky café, I seek out a sign,
The barista just chuckles, 'It's all just divine!'
The blend of my worries, espresso with cream,
Can caffeine awaken a whole new dream?

With each frothy swirl, I plan out my day,
But the sugar keeps distracting me, hey, 'What do they say?'
I gaze into my cup, it whispers and schemes,
Are my goals this year just a list of caffeine dreams?

A dash of cinnamon might help me decide,
Should I lead or follow, or just take a ride?
The steam from my latte reads like a cloud,
Telling me secrets, oh so very loud.

With a sip and a giggle, I sketch out my path,
Life's too short to ponder, bring on the wrath!
So raise up your mugs, let's toast to the beans,
For in this caffeinated world, we fulfill all our dreams!

In the Company of Foam

Surrounded by caffeine, I thrive in this space,
With foam-topped creations all over the place.
I strike up a chat with the frothy delight,
'Are you more of a latte, or a mocha tonight?'

The clock ticks away in a coffee shop haze,
As I sip on my dreams and lose track of days.
I laugh with the espresso, my loyal best mate,
In this bubble of joy, life's simply first-rate.

The pastries are teasing, their aromas so sweet,
But I choose just the coffee; I can't handle defeat.
With each little sip, I chuckle at fate,
As the world melts away — oh, isn't it great?

So here's to the foam, and the coffee that pours,
Let's celebrate chaos outside these four doors.
In the company of brews, any vision can form,
With laughter and caffeine, I'm always reborn!

Sip into the Day

Morning bells chime, I rise from my slumber,
My coffee machine roars, it's out for a number.
With a splash of the blend and a whirl of the grind,
I set out on missions with each little find.

The clock says it's early, but coffee screams 'Go!'
With every rich gulp, I'm ready to flow.
Do I conquer the world or just conquer this mug?
In the arena of caffeine, I give it a shrug.

The colors of cream swirl and dance in delight,
In this great daily battle, I'm ready to fight.
With my cup as my armor and humor my shield,
To the fields of adventure, I bravely will yield.

So cuddle your coffee, embrace all its charms,
With laughter and caffeine, it's love in our arms.
Let's sip into this day with glee and high fives,
For life's a grand journey and coffee revives!

Chase the Steam

A cup in hand, the morning call,
The world's a blur, I hear it all.
With every sip, I find my way,
Chasing steam to seize the day.

The mug is warm, my heart's ablaze,
In coffee's depths, I start to gaze.
The antics brew, I laugh and cheer,
Just give me caffeine, I have no fear!

Around the world, the beans parade,
Espresso shots, my plans are made.
With every gulp, I feel the light,
Who knew a brew could spark such delight?

So let's embrace this frothy dream,
Where laughter bubbles, nothing's extreme.
With friends, a brew, the world is fine,
Let's chase the steam, and feel divine!

Grounds of Intention

In the kitchen, chaos thrives,
The coffee grind, my quest derives.
A spoonful here, a dash of cheer,
With every sip, intentions clear.

I spill the beans, it's quite the mess,
Yet somehow still, I'm feeling blessed.
With each new blend, my mind takes flight,
Who knew life's answers brewed just right?

The grounds remind me of the quest,
To wake up early and feel the zest.
A frothy crown, my caffeine crown,
With every gulp, I won't back down!

So raise your mugs, let laughter flow,
In grounds of intention, we steal the show.
Life's mysteries wrapped in a cup,
Let's caffeinate and never give up!

Caffeine Dreams

Waking up, my mind's a blur,
Where'd my sanity occur?
A little jolt, a little swirl,
Enter caffeine, let's unfurl!

In every cup, a crazy scene,
Dancing beans, in caffeine dreams.
With every sip, I find my flair,
Why is the cat staring, I swear?

The morning muffin gives a wink,
"Hey buddy, time to think!"
But first, a brew, a toast to me,
Where's my spark? Ah, there's the tea!

So catch the drip, the magic flow,
Laugh out loud, let worries go.
In caffeine dreams, I find my scheme,
Together we'll brew, let's chase that dream!

Awakening the Soul

As dawn breaks through, I feel the pull,
A cup of joy, it fills me full.
With laughter brewing, I take a sip,
Awakening the soul with every trip.

The coffee pot sings a morning tune,
While sleepy heads come alive real soon.
A dash of cream, a sprinkle of fun,
With every brew, together we run!

The world awakens, joy in the air,
Friends gather round, we laugh and share.
With mugs raised high, we cheer our fate,
While caffeine's warmth leads us to create.

So let's embrace this morning dance,
With every cup, we take our chance.
Awakening the soul, let's feel the spark,
In funny moments, we make our mark!

Mornings of Mindfulness

I stumble to the kitchen, what a sight,
My hair's a mess, oh what a fright.
The kettle's loud, it has no shame,
But all this chaos feels like a game.

With every sip, my eyes wide awake,
I ponder life and all its flake.
Is coffee art? Or am I just mad?
In this moment, I'm both happy and sad.

When caffeine hits, I start to dance,
My mug's my partner in this wild romance.
A little foam, a little swirl,
Who knew mornings could provide such a whirl?

So here I am, all caffeinated bliss,
Finding joy in my morning miss.
Each cup a quest, each sip a thrill,
Perhaps, dear friend, I'll climb that hill.

Beyond the Bean.

In a world of grind, I search for fun,
My coffee's brewing; the day's begun.
The rich aroma hints at fate,
Can a mug really elevate?

With each dark drop, I'm feeling bold,
This potion's worth its weight in gold.
I ponder dreams with every taste,
Oh, this caffeine, it's no waste!

Spilling thoughts like Barbara's talk,
Do penguins sip? Do they even walk?
My cup is full of goofy doubt,
Yet in this nonsense, I find my route.

So here's to beans, the laughter's grind,
In steaming cups, our lives unwind.
Let's raise a toast to morning cheer,
For in the brew, purpose is clear.

Awakening in a Cup

I wake to find my mug's half full,
No time for silence, my heart's in a pull.
With each swig, my brain takes flight,
Is this the key to cosmic insight?

My coffee spills like endless dreams,
Dancing on counters, or so it seems.
I taste the hopes, the whims, the sighs,
In every drop, the universe lies.

Sugar swirls like a midday dance,
My spoon's a partner in this trance.
Am I a sage with a frothy dome?
Or just a weirdo who talks to foam?

So here's to mornings that make me grin,
In every sip, I know I'll win.
Let's laugh and slurp, make friends with luck,
For life's a journey; just sip and pluck.

The Brew of Intentions

With a splash and a pour, my day kicks off,
I'm the caffeine queen, no reason to scoff.
Stirring dreams with froth and foam,
In this mug, I find my home.

Sipping slowly, it's quite an art,
Brewing plans with a silly heart.
Do beans know secrets? Are they wise?
My heart races as I realize.

The world's awash in espresso gleam,
Is there a prize for the best coffee dream?
Each gulp's a quest, a grand charade,
In liquid joy, my worries fade.

So let the steam rise, let laughter soar,
My cup's a canvas, forever explore.
With every brew, I'll share the fun,
It's coffee magic, second to none!

Moments in the Mug

In a cup so warm and bright,
Dreams swirl like foam, just right.
Sips with a giggle, life takes flight,
Morning bliss, a pure delight.

Beneath the steam, my thoughts will race,
Each sip, a smile, a little grace.
Espresso shots, in this wild chase,
I ponder life, then spill my face.

With every brew, a tale unfolds,
Mug in hand, secrets told.
Laughter brews like coffee bold,
Moments shared, worth more than gold.

So raise your mug, embrace the cheer,
With every gulp, laughter near.
Life tastes better, have no fear,
Coffee friends make troubles disappear.

Awakening from a Dark Roast

Woke up grumpy, a cranky soul,
Dark roast ready to make me whole.
A jolt of joy fills up the bowl,
My hopes bubble like a caffeine goal.

The first sip hits—oh what a thrill,
Turning over a brand new hill.
Yesterday's woes seem so shrill,
With every drop, I feel the chill.

Dancing grounds in swirling steam,
Life pours out like a silly dream.
With laughter rising, a strong team,
I'm awake now—just hear me scream!

So here's to the beans that save the day,
Cheers to the chaos, I'll find my way.
In this little cup, come what may,
I'll brew my joy, come on, let's play!

Drip by Drip: Life's Lessons

Wake up to the drips and drops,
Life's a brew, let's make those hops.
In every cup, wisdom pops,
Sip carefully, no need for flops.

Each drop tells stories untold,
With a dash of milk, life's pure gold.
Stirring in laughter, smiling bold,
Lessons brewed hot, never cold.

Sometimes I spill, oh what a mess,
Life's a puzzle—let's confess.
With every drip, I must digress,
Find the joy in the coffee's press.

So grab your mug, let's cheer and cheer,
Each sip a lesson, far or near.
In this funny game, let's steer,
Coffee's got wisdom, sometimes unclear.

Percolated Insights

Brewed in bubbles, insights spill,
Every percolation, a little thrill.
With each swirl, the world's a quill,
Writing tales, warm and shrill.

Pour it slowly, don't rush the fun,
Life's lessons drip, one by one.
Like frothy cream in the morning sun,
Brewed to perfection, second to none.

So let's gawk at the steaming pot,
With every sip, what have we got?
A jolt of laughter, life's funny plot,
Insights crafted in every jot.

So here's to the brew, both strange and grand,
With giggles shared, together we stand.
Life's a percolation, isn't it planned?
With coffee in hand, it's all so unplanned!

Morning Blend Reflections

Woke up with a sleepy head,
The beans are brewing, dreams to spread.
I stir my thoughts, just like my cup,
With cream and sugar, I'll rise up!

The coffee's hot, it starts to shake,
Decisions made, no room for flake.
I sip and ponder, should I nap?
Or power through with this fine tap?

A dance of jitters, oh what fun,
My morning task cannot be done.
With each brisk gulp, my goals ignite,
I might just write that bestseller tonight!

The day's ahead, adventures wait,
Fueled by caffeine, oh, isn't fate great?
So here's to blends that clear my head,
Cheers to the coffee; to dreams, we're led!

Lattes and Life Lessons

I brewed a latte, frothy so bold,
It whispered secrets, stories untold.
With every swirl, a lesson learned,
Milk and espresso, my heart is churned.

Do I double shot? Or keep it light?
Decisions dance in the morning light.
Life's just like foam, it's here then it's gone,
Each sip a memory, raising the dawn.

Spilled a bit, oh what a mess!
Just like my plans, I must confess.
Yet laughter bubbles like froth on top,
A latte's life-lesson—never stop!

So I raise my cup to the skies above,
With laughter and caffeine, I'm full of love.
Sip by sip, I'll conquer the day,
Lattes in hand, I'm here to stay!

The Aroma of Aspiration

The aroma wafts, a fragrant spell,
Coffee dreams in a steaming shell.
I take a whiff, and soon I know,
This brewed ambition is set to flow.

A dash of nutmeg, a sprinkle of glee,
Goals and dreams, as rich as can be.
Each sip a nudge, a quirky cheer,
With every gulp, the path is clear.

I ponder life like a coffee bean,
Tossed, rolled, brewed, what will I glean?
Sip of determination, taste the zest,
With caffeine courage, I'm truly blessed!

So here's to mornings fresh and bright,
Where laughter brews and spirits ignite.
With each cup, aspirations steep,
In the world of coffee, there's treasure to reap!

Espresso Moments

An espresso shot, oh what a kick!
It jolts my senses, sharp and quick.
In tiny cups, big dreams abide,
Fueling thoughts I cannot hide.

With every sip, my mind takes flight,
Ideas bloom, oh what a sight!
Bittersweet, this brew of fate,
Moments like this, I can't wait!

Oh, a splash of chaos in my brew,
I laugh aloud, as I brew anew.
Life's espresso, a chance to savor,
With each rich gulp, I chase my flavor.

So here's to life, both frothy and strong,
Together we'll dance, we'll laugh along.
Espresso moments, oh what a thrill,
With coffee by my side, I'll climb that hill!

Flashes of Insight in Every Cup

A sip then a grin, my thoughts take a flight,
Ideas dance like sugar, a humorous sight.
With coffee in hand, oh what will I find?
A scheme for world peace or just snacks, never mind!

The barista just laughs, we share in the cream,
As I ponder my life like it's all a big dream.
Eureka! I shout, then spill on my shirt,
My genius is messy, but laughter won't hurt!

A frothy concoction, all bubbling with cheer,
Turns problems to jokes, like they disappear.
I'm serious, really, I'm deep in thought here,
But with each silly sip, I just can't help but cheer!

So raise up your cup, let's toast to the morn,
Where brains meet the brew and great thoughts are born.
In my caffeinated quest, I know that it's true,
With laughter and foam, there's nothing we can't do!

The Heart of a Good Brew

Pour me a cup that's bold and sincere,
Each drop tells a tale, oh lend me your ear!
The steam from the pot whispers stories untold,
Of cookies and laughter, both brash and bold.

The beans had a journey, a trip near and far,
To land in my mug, a caffeinated star.
I sip and I muse, each gulp full of cheer,
For wisdom's just waiting right here in the sphere!

A splash of dark chocolate, a dash of sweet spice,
This brew's got a heartbeat; oh isn't it nice?
I stir up the thoughts with a spoon that's quite witty,
To chat with my coffee, oh isn't that pretty?

So here's to the blend, rich, hearty, and fine,
Each mug is a heart, and with yours, I'll combine.
Together we'll laugh, over sips we align,
In this steaming hot symphony, we'll surely shine!

From Grounds to Greatness

From grounds in the pot to the cup in my hand,
The journey is funny — oh isn't it grand?
I grind up my worries, I brew up some glee,
Transforms all my thoughts into liquid esprit!

The coffee drips down like a gentle rain,
Each drop's little giggle eases my brain.
I ponder my purpose, then chuckle aloud,
Maybe I'll start a band, instead of feeling proud!

I add way too much cream, it's a frothy mishap,
Maybe I'll stick with this coffee-shop map.
With each sip I take, the world's a great play,
Just me and my coffee, we laugh all the way!

So here's to the grind, the percolate cheer,
Each mugful's a nugget of joy, that's quite clear.
Let's celebrate each cup, the great and the small,
For in the world of coffee, we're having a ball!

Stirred Thoughts Over Coffee

With spoon in my hand, I start to reflect,
Each swirl of my drink, ideas I collect.
I stir up my dreams, oh what a delight,
As my coffee concoction dances in the light!

The caffeine whirls through, igniting my muse,
In this frothy elixir, I lightheartedly choose.
A sprinkle of chaos, a dash of good fun,
With each steady sip, my worries come undone!

I ponder the meaning of life over lattes,
While creating wild plans, like hosting parades.
A quiche at my side, the world feels just right,
In the kingdom of caffeine, it's a whimsical sight!

So let's raise our cups, to laughter and glee,
With every hot sip, there's more jubilee.
For in the world of our mugs, clever thoughts regularly do brew,
And every stir deepens the bond between me and you!

Morning Brew Revelations

With beans aglow, the morning wakes,
I sip and ponder my life's mistakes.
The mug spills thoughts, oh what a splurge,
In frothy dreams, my hopes emerge.

The barista winks, a devilish tease,
Says caffeine magic brings you to your knees.
I laugh and choke on my big latte,
Wishing I had just made a parfait.

Each sip's a chance, each gulp a lore,
What am I here for? Oh, who knows more!
A foam mustache starts to rise,
I'm still a mess under coffee skies.

Pouring courage into my cup,
With every gulp I feel a puff.
So here's to brews that brighten my day,
Who needs a plan? Just brew away!

Sips of Solace

In a café nook with a comfy chair,
I drown my woes, beyond compare.
My mug's my therapist, rich and hot,
Stirring up thoughts I forgot I had bought.

The sugar pours like my wild dreams,
I taste the sweetness, hear the screams.
Caffeine helps me embrace the dread,
Those thoughts can brew while I share bread.

Uh-oh, here comes the dark roast grin,
Life's just a brew, let the fun begin!
With every sip, I grow a bit wise,
Or so I think, with caffeine-tinted eyes.

I sip my fate, with cream on top,
Hoping this ride won't come to a stop.
Though spills may come, it's all in jest,
A sip of solace, I'll take my best!

The Espresso Quest

Adventure calls, oh glorious brew,
With a tiny shot, I bid adieu.
I chase the espresso, not far, just near,
Through frothy towns and mugs full of cheer.

A map made of beans leads the way,
Each café corner, a place to stay.
I slay my grind, a warrior bold,
Plundering lattes and tales retold.

At each stop, a tale to hack,
My coffee wisdom starts to stack.
"Next stop, happiness!" I shout with glee,
As baristas nod and chuckle with me.

To brew or not, that is the plight,
Kings of caffeine will join tonight.
So raise your cups, let's conquer this quest,
For every sip is a jolly jest!

Whispers in a Cup

In ceramic walls, whispers speak,
Stories of mornings, quirky and meek.
Each swirl of steam a secret to share,
Brewed truths bubble up, beyond compare.

A custard surprise in my pastry slice,
"Why am I here?" I ponder precise.
A coffee sip and a cheeky grin,
Turns my frown into mischief within.

The daily grind, oh what a joke,
My cup of joy spills, oh how I choke!
At tables round, the laughter flows,
In this coffee shop, anything goes.

So here's to the whispers in each brew,
Where laughter bubbles and silly dreams brew.
With each sip, a reason to smile,
Let's stir the world, one fun cup at a while!

A Symphony of Flavors

With each cup, a tune does play,
A melody in beans so fray.
Espresso notes, bold and bright,
Sipped so deep, it feels just right.

Froth like clouds, steamed and swirled,
Each sip's a dance, a flavor twirled.
A sprinkle here, a dash of glee,
In coffee's arms, I'm wild and free.

Dark roast dreams, a nightly fate,
I laugh at those who hesitate.
For in this brew, joy finds its way,
Java smiles, brightening the day.

So raise your mugs, a cheerful cheer,
For every sip, a laugh is near.
In flavors rich, we find our jive,
Together, let's brew, and come alive!

Brewed Awakening

Mornings are tough, but I have my hack,
A magical potion, in a little black sack.
With each drip, my eyelids rise,
Caffeine's the answer, oh what a surprise!

Found a grind that steals my woes,
A cup of joy where the laughter flows.
From beans that dance to mugs that sing,
Every sip's a giggle—oh, what a fling!

The coffee shop's my favorite stage,
Where latte art writes a bubbly page.
The barista's jokes as frothy as foam,
In this warm cup, I feel right at home.

So here's to the brew, my liquid muse,
Each cup a story, I simply can't refuse.
In every drop, I find my spark,
My morning ritual lights up the dark!

The Essence of Each Sip

A sip of bliss on a dreary day,
My troubles vanish, they float away.
Steeped in warmth, with a hint of fun,
This coffee magic, oh how I run!

Ceramic hugs in every pour,
Drizzle of cream, I always want more.
Beneath the surface, rich laughter brews,
Every sip's a chance to choose!

It's nectar for dreams, a wild ride,
Each cup a smile, often tried.
From bitter to sweet, I take a dive,
In each little sip, I feel alive.

So fill my cup, let it overflowing,
With java joy, oh it's worth knowing.
With every taste, I learn to play,
In this simple drink, I find my way!

Coffee Chronicles

In the land of beans, adventures unfold,
A tale of joy worth more than gold.
From mochas to lattes, the journey's grand,
With every cup, a new story planned.

A splash of sugar, and a frothy dance,
Coffee whispers secrets, if you take a chance.
Quirky flavors that tickle the mind,
As I sip, more hilarity to find.

Barista winks, serves with flair,
I raise my cup, free from despair.
In every gulp, a twist awaits,
Each coffee moment, the fates create.

So join the quest in this vibrant brew,
Where laughter reigns and joy is true.
Each cup a chapter, together we play,
In this coffee chronicle, we find our way!

Beans of Brilliance

In a cup I see my dreams,
Full of froth and chocolate beams.
Stirring chaos with a spoon,
Who knew caffeine's such a boon?

With each sip my worries fade,
Capturing goals I thought betrayed.
A jolt of joy, a twist of fate,
I'll conquer worlds—oh, wait, it's late!

Roasted visions dance and swirl,
Java jests as life does twirl.
Each bean a tale, a laugh, a cheer,
In this mug, my dreams are near!

So here's to cups that brew delight,
Fueling antics by day and night.
With beans of brilliance in my hand,
I brew success, and it's quite grand!

Finding Myself in a Mocha

I stumbled in, my hair a mess,
A mocha's warmth in my distress.
With whipped cream clouding my deep thoughts,
I ponder dreams and accidental slots.

Chocolaty whispers call my name,
This drink's a wild, delicious game.
I spill a little, laugh, and grin,
My deepest plots now swirled within!

As chocolate flows, so does my mind,
Mild absurdities I now find.
The world transforms with every sip,
Reality's gone on a short trip!

So bring on sprinkles, bring on the fun,
With each rich taste, I've surely won!
In frothy layers my dreams reside,
Finding myself, in cream, I glide!

The Pour of Possibility

I take my cup, the morning's glow,
With every pour, my ideas flow.
Milk and espresso swirl and twirl,
Creating wonders, oh what a whirl!

Each drop, a dream that's set to rise,
Like foamy clouds in sunny skies.
Spilling beans, I chuckle in glee,
Life's a barista, and oh, it's free!

A latte art that's far from plain,
Makes me think, perhaps I should paint!
Crafting visions with frothy flair,
The pour of life is beyond compare!

So raise your mugs, let's toast a cheer,
For every pour releases a fear.
In cups, we find what's truly real,
With every sip, we learn to feel!

Chasing Shadows with Steamy Lattes

In shadows cast by morning light,
I chase my whims with mugs in sight.
Steamy lattes whisper sweet dreams,
As I plot mischief with silly schemes!

A frothy heart, it giggles wide,
Holding secrets that must collide.
Milk mustache on my upper lip,
Life's a carnival, a frothy trip!

With every sip, I start to see,
That laughter's what will set me free.
In flavors rich, my heart takes flight,
Chasing shadows till the night!

So gather round, my caffeinated crew,
With chocolate drizzles and coffee too.
We'll chase delight, one cup at a time,
For in each swirl, there's joy sublime!

www.ingramcontent.com/pod-product-compliance
Lightning Source LLC
Chambersburg PA
CBHW051636160426
43209CB00004B/670